Brown's Star Atlas, Showing all the Bright Stars, With Full Instructions how to Find and use Them for Navigational Purposes and Board of Trade Examinations ..

BROWN'S
STAR ATLAS,

SHOWING ALL THE BRIGHT STARS,

WITH

FULL INSTRUCTIONS HOW TO FIND AND USE THEM

FOR

NAVIGATIONAL 'PURPOSES

AND

BOARD OF TRADE EXAMINATIONS.

[*Entered at Stationers' Hall*]

GLASGOW

JAMES BROWN & SON, Nautical and Engineering Publishers

London SIMPKIN, MARSHALL, HAMILTON, KENT & CO, Ltd

1904

PREFACE.

RECENT YEARS have witnessed a considerable development of interest in Stellar Navigation. This is due in some measure to the fact that it now forms an important feature of the Board of Trade examinations, but both the increased interest and its inclusion in the examinations are results of the further fact that its importance and necessity are becoming more clearly recognised, and that it is now acknowledged to be an essential factor in the navigation of modern vessels

This atlas is intended for the use and guidance of those who wish to be able to recognise the principal BRIGHT stars, and to become proficient star navigators, and while it is of interest to those going up for examination, it is essentially a book for practical use at sea

PART I is designed to help beginners to trace out the principal constellations and BRIGHT stars The six large maps show all the BRIGHT stars projected on the plane of a meridian, and may be used by observers in any latitude A study of these maps not only facilitates the recognition of the stars, but also fixes in the mind an approximate knowledge of their positions in the heavens, and of the times when they are available for observation The fact that the maps are continuous, and show in unbroken succession all the BRIGHT stars, is believed to be a good feature In addition to this the principal constellations are further illustrated on special maps The maps have been drawn by Mr DENNING, F R A S

PART II deals with the use of the stars in practical navigation, and the various methods of finding a ship's position, and the deviation of the compass are explained

A E. NICHOLLS, EXTRA MASTER,

HONOURS MEDALLIST IN NAUTICAL ASTRONOMY

CONTENTS.

PART I —HOW TO FIND THE STARS.

PART II.—STAR PROBLEMS.

PART I.

HOW TO FIND THE STARS.

Explanation of the maps, and directions for tracing and recognising the principal constellations and bright stars.

THE MAPS are designed in such a manner that sections of the heavens are presented for observation in rotation

On each map the central portion is the part specially presented for study, and is printed with white stars on a dark ground, this being most striking to the eye Each of these sections shows a portion of the heavens from Pole to Pole, included between Meridians, 4 hours or 60° apart. The whole firmament thus occupies six maps

On each side of these sections, for convenience of reference, the stars in the adjacent regions of the heavens are shown To avoid overcrowding the maps, only the brighter stars, or those used in navigation, appear

The observer must imagine himself to be holding the map overhead and looking at it from below, the North point of the map being directed to the North The central North and South line then represents the meridian, and he will easily understand that the right hand half of each map represents the Western part of the heavens, and the left hand portion the Eastern part

It is not possible to represent the celestial sphere on a plane surface such as a map, and at the same time to preserve the relative distances and bearings of all the stars from each other   In all maps of the stars there must be a certain amount of distortion or misplacement , only on a globe can their relative positions be accurately illustrated   In the method of projection here chosen the apparent misplacement is least in the central portion of the maps, and this is the reason that attention is directed to that part.   Otherwise the whole heavens might have been presented on two maps only.

As the position of a place on the earth's surface is fixed by its *Latitude* and *Longitude*, so the position of a point in the celestial sphere is fixed by its *Right Ascension* and *Declination*

The Declination of any object is its angular distance North or South of the Equinoctial or Celestial Equator, measured along the meridian   It thus corresponds to *Latitude* on the earth's surface   On the maps the Equinoctial is the line through the centre from East to West

The Right Ascension of a celestial object is the arc of the Equinoctial between the first point of Aries and the meridian of the object, always reckoning eastward from the first point of Aries   It thus corresponds to *Longitude* on the earth, but differs in the manner in which it is reckoned , for, whilst longitude is reckoned East and West of the meridian of Greenwich, Right Ascension is reckoned in only one direction, viz, eastward from o to 24 hours, or 360°   Therefore, when we say a star's Right Ascension is 2 hours, or 13 hours, etc , we mean that it is on a meridian 2 hours or 13 hours, etc , East of the first point of Aries   It is usual to express R A in time, and, when looking South, R A will increase to the left   On the large maps meridians are drawn for each hour

NOTE—The first point of Aries is the point where the sun's centre crosses the Equinoctial when passing from South to North Declination   It is not marked in the heavens by any star   On Map I it is indicated by the point on the Equinoctial where the o or 24 hours meridian crosses it

Naming of Stars.

Constellations.—A Constellation consists of a number of stars grouped under one name These names have been handed down from the earliest days of astronomy The stars belonging to a constellation are distinguished by prefixing to each one a letter of the Greek alphabet Thus we have α Orionis, β Orionis, α Ursæ Majoris, etc The constellation names are printed in capitals on the maps Some of the principal constellations are also shown on special maps, with the Greek letters attached to each star

In addition to the above style of distinguishing stars most of the principal stars have been given proper names, thus *α Orionis* is also named BETELGUESE, *α Ursæ Majoris* is known as DUBHE, and so on These names are printed on the maps in smaller type, but only the more familiar ones have been given, so as to avoid overcrowding the maps with names A full list of the names will be found on page 4

Magnitudes of Stars.

The magnitude or brilliancy of each star is indicated by a number, and the brighter the star, the less this number will be The magnitude numbers are now given to tenths, that is, to one decimal figure (*see* Table of Stars), and a star of magnitude 1·5 is one-tenth of a magnitude brighter than one of magnitude 1 6

Two of the stars are so bright that their magnitudes are denoted by minus numbers, as they are brighter than magnitude o Sirius, the brightest of the fixed stars, is of magnitude − 1 4. Canopus is next in brilliancy with magnitude − 1 o.

Stars that do not rise above the Observer's Horizon.

If an observer's *latitude* and a star's *declination* have *different names* and their *sum exceeds 90°*, the star will not rise above the horizon in that latitude This can

Mean Right Ascension and Declination of Fixed Stars for January 1, 1904, and maps on which they appear.

	Star's Name.	Mag	Right Ascension			Annual Change		Declination			Annual Change.
			h	m	s	s		°	′	″	″
STARS ON MAP I	α Andromedæ (Alpherat),	2 1	0	3	25	+ 3	N	28	33	38	+ 20
	γ Pegasi (Algenib),	2 9	0	8	17	− 3	N	14	39	0	+ 20
	β Ceti (Diphda),	2 2	0	38	46	· 3	S	18	30	48	+ 20
	β Andromedæ (Mirach),	2 4	1	4	21	⊤ 3	N	35	6	42	+ 19
	α Ursæ Min (Polaris),	2 1	1	24	16	⊤ 26	N	88	47	42	+ 19
	α Eridani (Achernar),	0 5	1	34	8	− 2	S	57	43	28	+ 18
	α Arietis (Hamal),	2 2	2	1	46	+ 3	N	23	0	31	+ 17
	α Ceti (Menkar),	2 8	2	57	16	+ 3	N	3	42	48	+ 14
	β Persei (Algol),	(var)	3	1	55	± 4	N	40	35	10	+ 14
	α Persei (Mirfak),	1 9	3	17	28	⊹ 4	N	49	31	12	+ 13
STARS ON MAP II	α Tauri (Aldebaran),	1 1	4	30	25	+ 3	N	16	19	0	+ 8
	α Aurigæ (Capella),	0 2	5	9	36	+ 4	N	45	54	3	+ 4
	β Orionis (Rigel),	c 3	5	9	55	+ 3	S	8	18	44	+ 4
	γ Orionis (Bellatrix),	1 7	5	19	59	+ 3	N	6	15	47	+ 3
	β Tauri (Nath),	1 8	5	20	13	+ 4	N	28	31	36	+ 3
	ε Orionis (Alnilam),	1 7	5	31	21	+ 3	S	1	15	46	+ 2
	ζ Orionis (Alnitak),	2 0	5	35	55	+ 3	S	1	59	35	+ 2
	α Orionis (Betelgeuse),	(var)	5	49	58	+ 3	N	7	23	22	+ 1
	η Geminorum,	(var)	6	9	5	+ 4	N	22	32	6	− 1
	α Argûs (Canopus),	− 1 0	6	21	49	+ 1	S	52	38	35	− 2
	α Canis Majoris (Sirius),	− 1 4	6	40	55	⊣ 3	S	16	35	2	− 4
	ε Canis Majoris (Adara),	1 6	6	54	51	+ 2	S	28	50	28	− 5
	δ Canis Majoris (Wezen),	2 0	7	4	29	+ 2	S	26	14	26	− 6
	α² Geminorum (Castor),	2 0	7	28	29	+ 4	N	32	5	59	− 8
	α Canis Min (Procyon),	0 5	7	34	17	⊢ 3	N	5	28	15	− 8
	β Geminorum (Pollux),	1 2	7	39	27	⊤ 4	N	28	15	30	− 8
STARS ON MAP III	ε Argûs,	1 7	8	20	33	+ 1	S	59	12	2	− 12
	δ Argûs,	2 0	8	42	3	⊣ 2	S	54	21	24	− 13
	λ Argûs,	1 7	9	12	9	+ 1	S	69	19	18	− 15
	α Hydræ (Alphard),	2 2	9	22	52	+ 3	S	8	14	32	− 16
	α Leonis (Regulus),	1 3	10	3	16	⊣ 3	N	12	26	12	− 18
	α Ursæ Majoris (Dubhe),	2 0	10	57	49	+ 4	N	62	16	10	− 19
	β Leonis (Denebola),	2 2	11	44	10	+ 3	N	15	6	31	− 20
	γ Ursæ Majoris (Phecda),	2 5	11	48	47	+ 3	N	54	13	43	− 20
STARS ON MAP IV	α¹ Crucis (Southern Cross),	1 0	12	21	15	+ 3	S	62	34	1	− 20
	γ Centauri,	2 4	12	36	13	+ 3	S	48	25	58	− 20
	β Crucis,	1 5	12	42	6	+ 3	S	59	9	51	− 20
	ε Ursæ Majoris (Alioth),	1 8	12	49	48	+ 3	N	56	28	51	− 20
	α Virginis (Spica),	1 2	13	20	8	+ 3	S	10	39	37	− 19
	η Ursæ Majoris (Benetnasch),	1 9	13	43	46	+ 2	N	49	47	32	− 18
	β Centauri,	0 8	13	57	3	+ 4	S	59	54	36	− 17
	θ Centauri,	2 1	14	1	2	+ 4	S	35	53	52	− 17
	α Boötis (Arcturus),	0 3	14	11	17	+ 3	N	19	40	55	− 17
	α² Centauri,	1	14	33	5	+ 5	S	60	26	13	− 16
	β Ursæ Minoris (Kochab),	2 2	14	50	59	− 0	N	74	32	52	− 15
	β Libræ (Zubenelg),	2 8	15	11	50	+ 3	S	9	1	44	− 13
	α Coronæ (Alphacca),	2 3	15	30	37	+ 3	N	27	2	15	− 12
	α Serpen is (Unuk),	2 8	15	39	32	+ 3	N	6	43	39	− 12
	δ Scorpii,	2 5	15	54	39	⊢ 4	S	22	20	56	− 10
STARS ON MAP V	α Scorpii (Antares),	1 3	16	23	31	+ 4	S	26	13	9	− 8
	α Triang Aust,	1 9	16	38	30	+ 6	S	68	51	7	− 7
	ε Scorpii,	2 3	16	43	57	⊣ 4	S	34	7	10	− 7
	η Ophiuchi,	2 6	17	4	52	+ 3	S	15	36	23	− 5
	λ Scorpii,	1 8	17	27	5	+ 4	S	37	2	2	− 3
	α Ophiuchi (Ras al Hague)	2 1	17	30	29	+ 3	N	12	37	46	− 3
	α Sagittarii (Kaus Australis),	1 9	18	17	48	+ 4	S	34	25	49	+ 2
	α Lyræ (Vega),	0 1	18	33	41	+ 2	N	38	41	39	+ 3
	σ Sagittarii,	2 1	18	49	19	+ 4	S	26	24	59	+ 4
	α Aquilæ (Altair),	0 9	19	46	6	+ 3	N	8	36	52	+ 9
STARS ON MAP VI	α Pavonis,	2 0	20	18	3	+ 5	S	57	2	35	+ 11
	α Cygni (Deneb),	1 3	20	38	10	+ 2	N	44	56	13	+ 13
	α Cephei (Alderamin),	2 6	21	16	17	+ 1	N	62	10	43	+ 15
	ε Pegasi (Enif),	2 5	21	39	28	⊣ 3	N	9	26	5	+ 16
	α Gruis,	1 9	22	2	11	+ 4	S	47	25	34	+ 17
	α Pis Aus. (Fomalhaut),	1 3	22	52	21	+ 3	S	30	7	52	+ 19
	α Pegasi (Markab),	2 6	22	56	59	+ 3	N	14	41	19	+ 19

be seen by inspection from the maps, as the parallels are drawn for every 10°, therefore, if from the observer's latitude to the position of the star is over 90°, it will not appear above his horizon

Stars that are always above the Horizon, or Circumpolar Stars.

If the observer's *latitude* and a star's *declination* have the *same name* and their *sum exceeds* 90°, that star will *always* be above the horizon, describing a circle round the elevated pole of the heavens

The two last rules may conveniently be put thus —subtract your latitude from 90 and thus get the co-latitude *All stars in the opposite hemisphere with declination greater than the co-latitude will not rise above the horizon, and all stars in the same hemisphere with declination greater than co-latitude will be circumpolar, that is, will describe a circle round the pole always above the horizon.*

In London (latitude about 51½° N, co-latitude 38½°) all stars in the Southern Hemisphere with declination greater than 38½° will always be below the horizon, and all stars in the Northern Hemisphere with declination greater than 38½° will be circumpolar It must be noted here that stars seldom become visible until 5° or so above the horizon

On the following page is a Table giving the times on certain dates when the stars on the central portion of each map are near the meridian Every day each star crosses the meridian about 4 minutes earlier than on the preceding day, that is, roughly, about 2 hours earlier per month Stars, therefore, which are near the meridian on any date, will occupy the same position about 2 hours earlier on the same day of the following month

When comparing the maps with the sky, regard must be had to the observer's latitude, and to the rules for stars above the horizon as given

Table showing the times when the stars on each map are near the meridian on certain dates.

	4hrs A M	2hrs A M	MIDNIGHT	10hrs P M	8hrs P M
Map I	August 22	September 22	October 22	November 22	December 22
,, II	October ,	November ,,	December ,,	January ,,	February ,,
,, III	December ,,	January ,,	February ,,	March ,,	April ,,
,, IV	February ,,	March ,,	April ,,	May ,,	June ,,
,, V	April ,	May ,,	June ,,	July ,,	August ,,
,, VI	June ,,	July ,,	August ,,	September ,,	October ,,

From the above Table the student should not have much difficulty in selecting the particular maps which show the stars near the meridian at any time of the day throughout the year

MAP I.

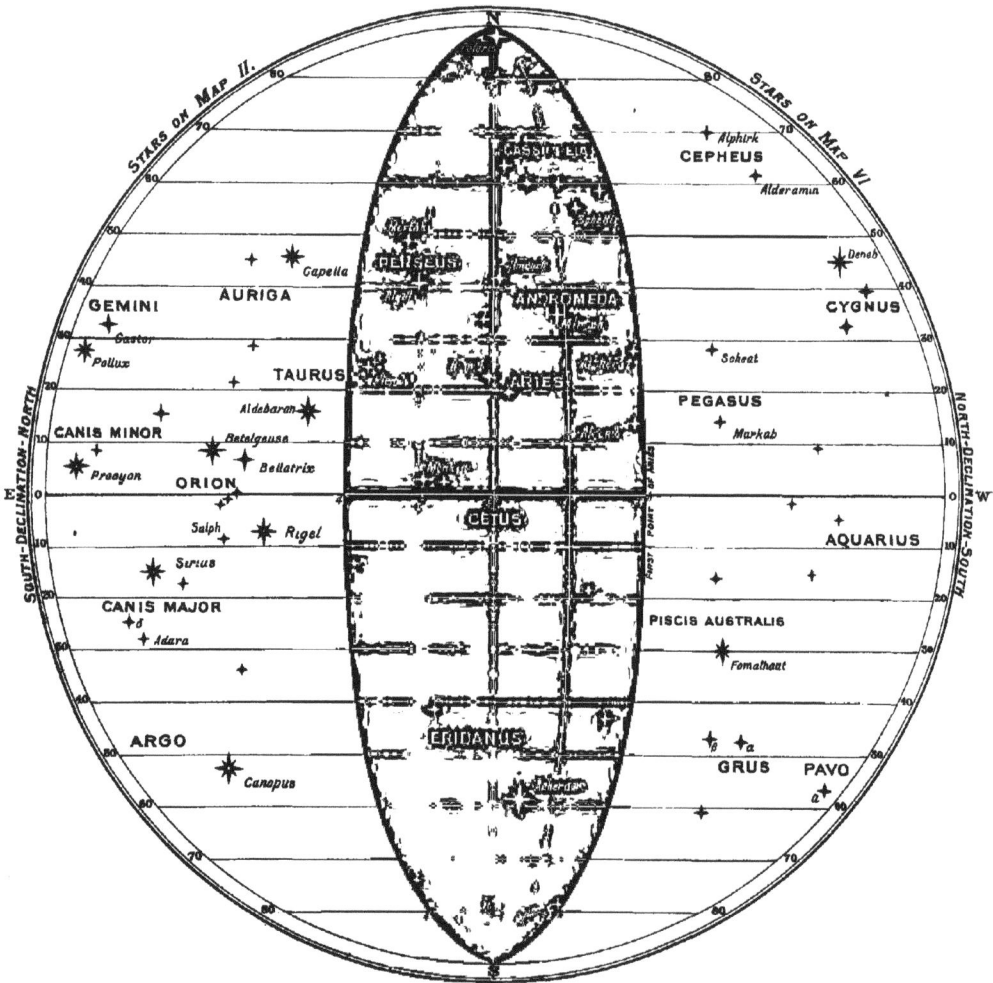

N

Polaris

STARS ON MAP II.

STARS ON MAP VI.

CASSIOPEIA

CEPHEUS

Alphirk

Alderamin

PERSEUS

Capella

AURIGA

ANDROMEDA

Denab

GEMINI

CYGNUS

Castor

Pollux

TAURUS

ARIES

Scheat

PEGASUS

CANIS MINOR

Aldebaran

Betelgeuse

Markab

Procyon

Bellatrix

ORION

SOUTH-DECLINATION-NORTH

E

Saiph

Rigel

CETUS

Sirius

AQUARIUS

NORTH-DECLINATION-SOUTH

W

CANIS MAJOR

PISCIS AUSTRALIS

δ

Adara

Fomalhaut

ARGO

ERIDANUS

β *α*

Canopus

GRUS

PAVO

α

The Central Portion shows the Stars between R A Ohrs (or 24hrs), and R A 4hrs
Towards the end of October they will be near the Meridian at Midnight, and in the eastern part of the sky about 8 p m

MAP II.

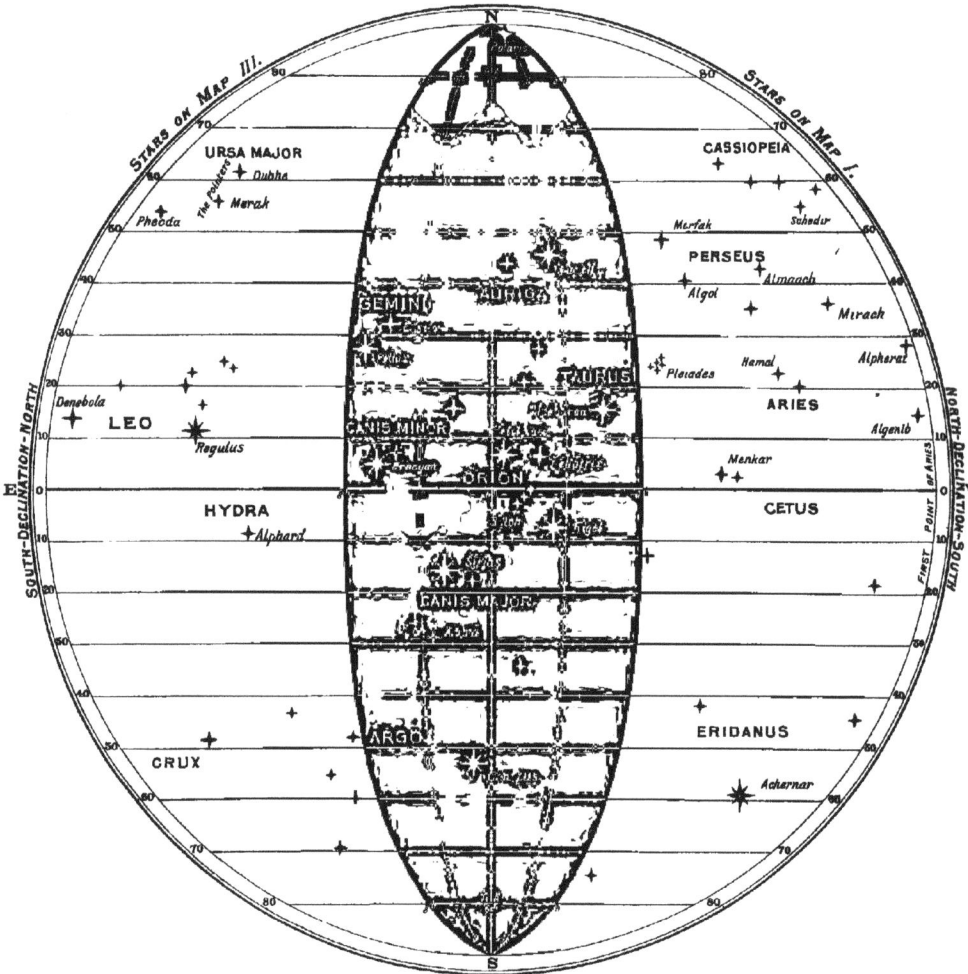

The Central Portion shows the Stars between R A 4hrs and R A 8hrs
Towards the end of December they will be near the Meridian at Midnight, and in the eastern part of the sky at 8 p m

MAP V.

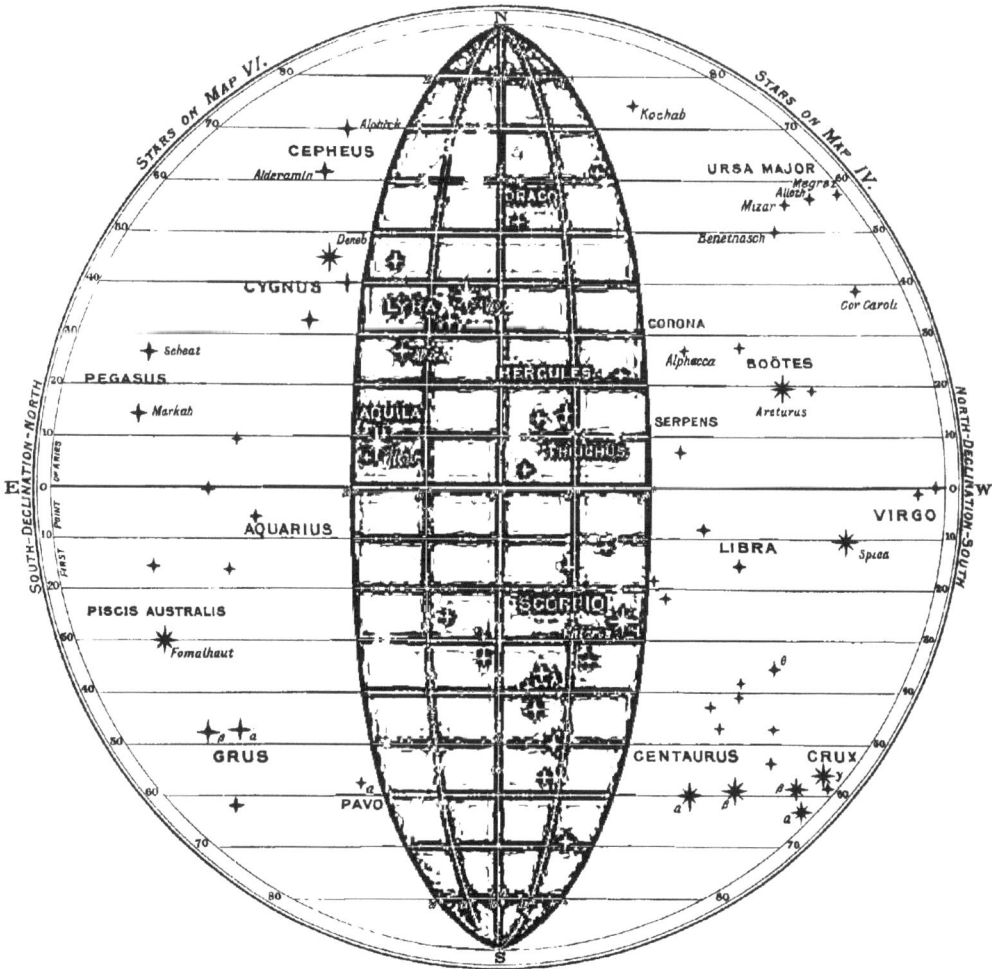

The Central Portion shows the Stars between R.A. 16hrs and R.A 20hrs
Towards the end of June they will be near the Meridian at Midnight, and in the eastern part of the sky at 8 p.m.

MAP IV.

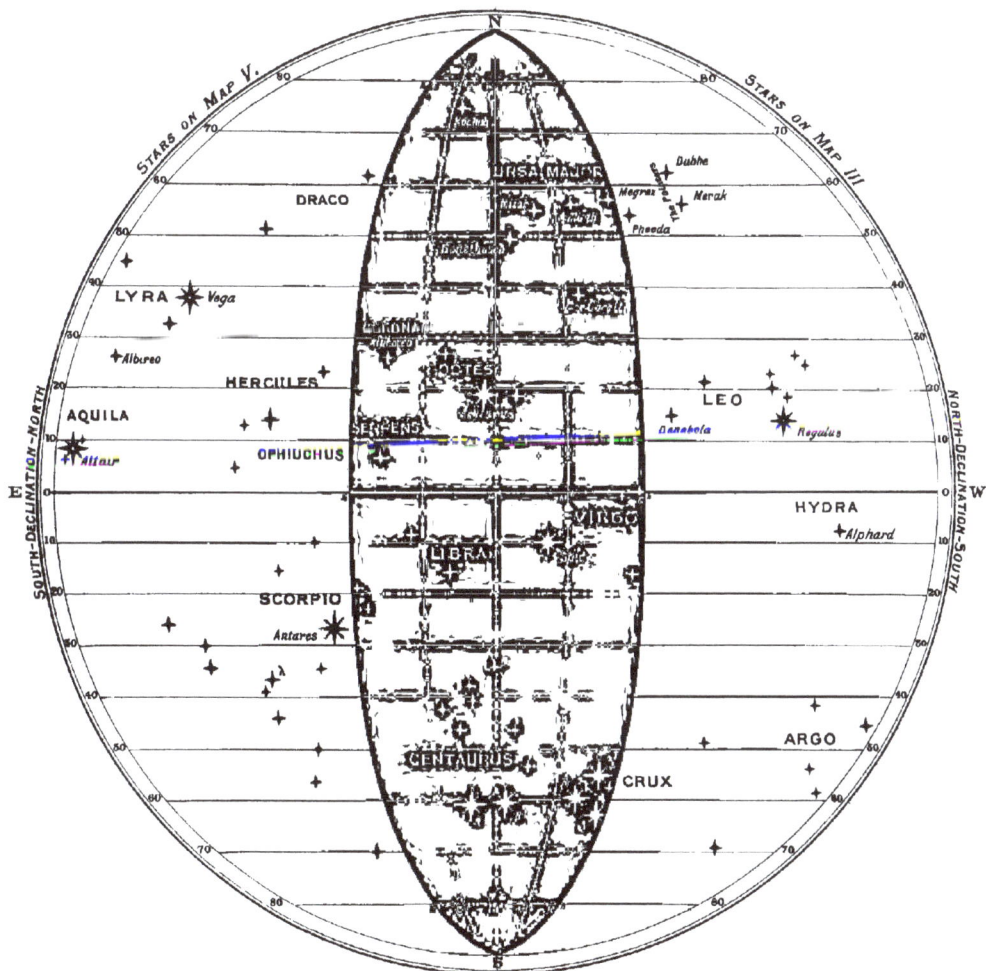

N

STARS ON MAP V.

STARS ON MAP III

DRACO

Dubhe

URSA MAJOR

Megrez   Merak

Mizar

Phecda

LYRA   Vega

Alcor

HERCULES

LEO

AQUILA

Denebola

Regulus

SERPENS

Altair

OPHIUCHUS

SOUTH-DECLINATION-NORTH

NORTH-DECLINATION-SOUTH

E   W

VIRGO

HYDRA

Alphard

LIBRA

SCORPIO

Antares

ARGO

CENTAURUS

CRUX

S

The Central Portion shows the Stars between R A 12hrs and R A 18hrs
Towards the end of April they will be near the Meridian at Midnight, and in the eastern part of the sky at 8 p m

MAP III.

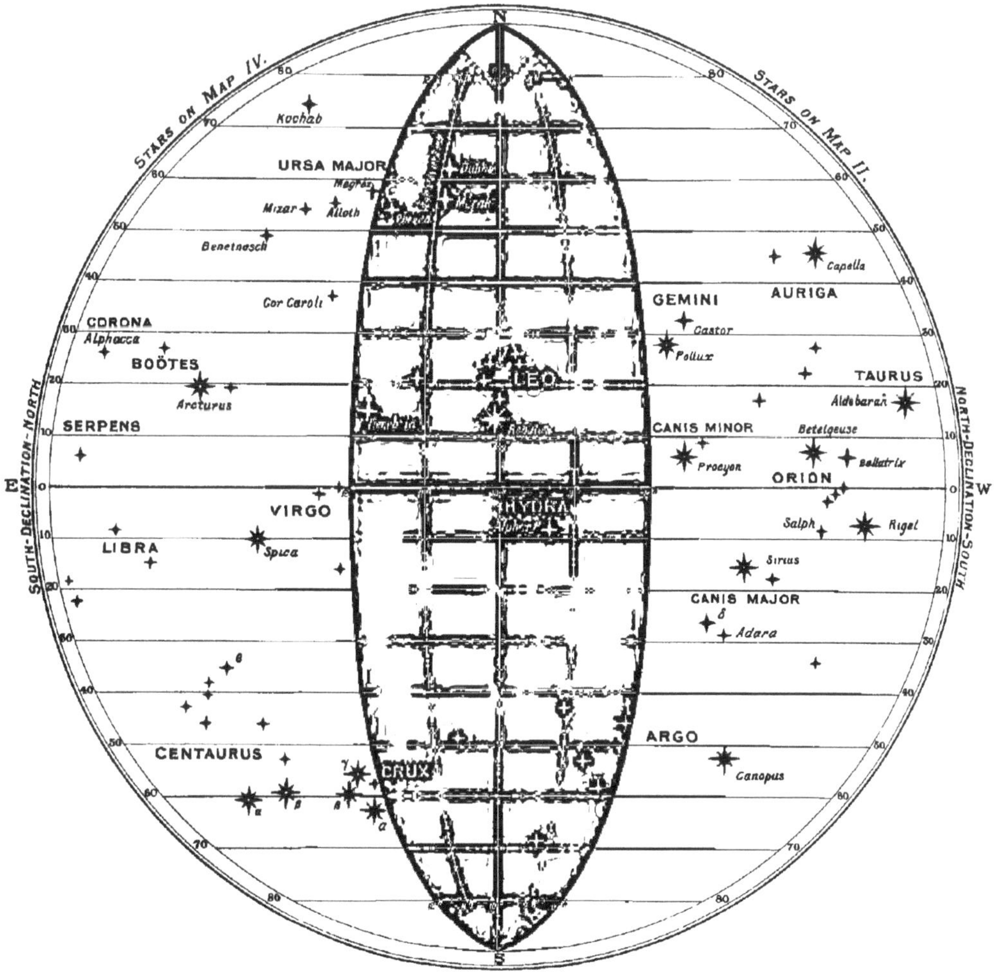

MAP VI.

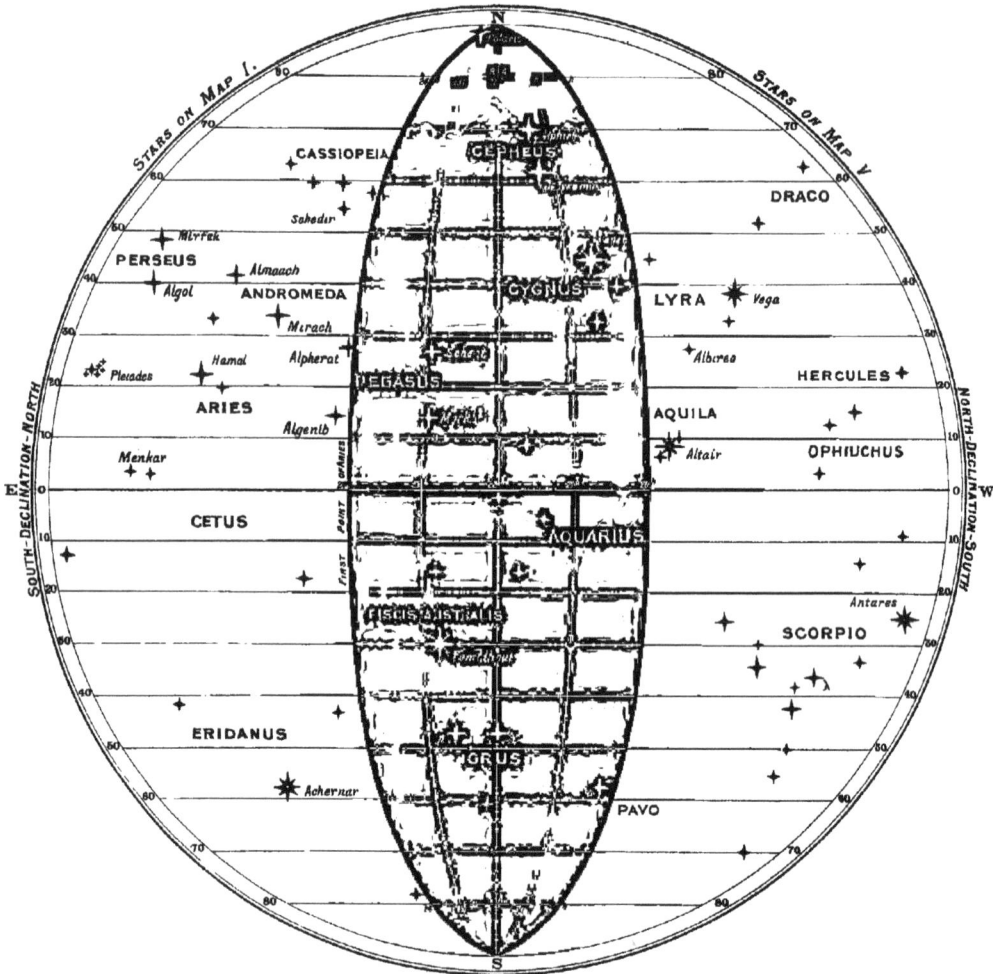

The Central Portion shows the Stars between R.A. 20hrs and R.A. 24hrs.
Towards the end of August they will be near the Meridian at Midnight, and in the eastern part of the sky at 8 p.m.

How to trace the Principal Constellations and Bright Stars.

No attempt will be made here to confuse the mind of the reader with long and elaborate directions It will be sufficient to briefly indicate how the principal bright stars in the various constellations may be identified With the position of these established in his mind as leading marks in different parts of the heavens, methods of distinguishing or tracing others will suggest themselves to the observer as he studies the stars in the sky

URSA MAJOR
(The Great Bear).

It will be convenient to begin with this constellation It is specially illustrated on the adjoining small map To observers in a higher latitude than about 45° N, this constellation is always visible on clear nights, being circumpolar The two stars α (or *Dubhe*) and β (or *Merak*) are called the "Pointers," because they point almost directly to the North Star

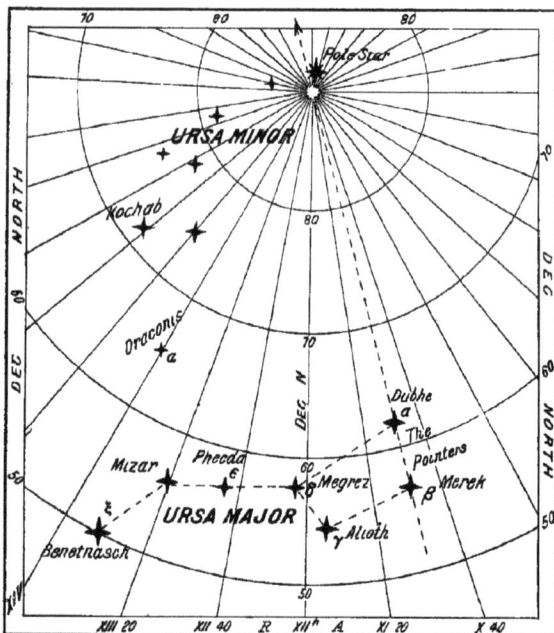

See also Large Maps III and IV

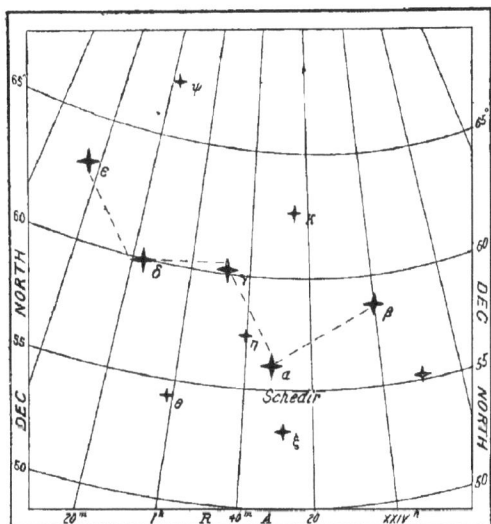

See also Large Map I

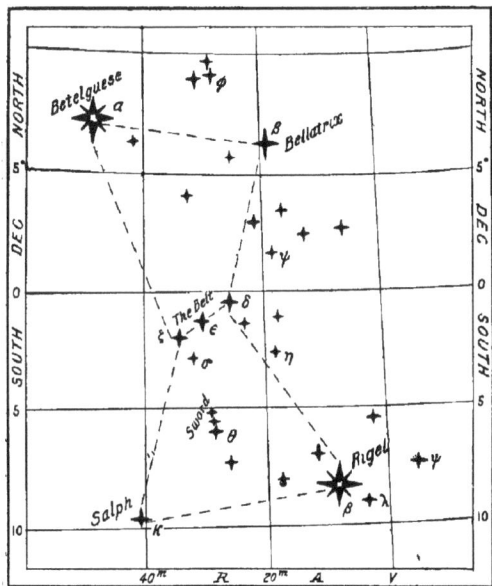

See also Large Map II

CASSIOPEIA.

On the opposite side of the Pole Star, but a little nearer to it than Ursa Major, is the smaller constellation CASSIOPEIA, also visible on all clear nights to observers in a higher North latitude than 45° When URSA MAJOR is above the Pole Star CASSIOPEIA is below it, and *vice versa*

To obtain a view of these constellations as they appear when below the Pole, hold the small maps straight before you, facing North, instead of overhead

ORION.

The most casual observer of the stars could not fail to notice this constellation when visible The stars forming it lie on both sides of the Equinoctial, and within 10° of it, They therefore rise well above the horizon in all navigable latitudes The three smaller stars in line with each other just South of the Equinoctial are called "Orion's Belt"

In line with these, and nearly equidistant in opposite directions, are the bright stars *Aldebaran* and *Sirius* (*see* large map II)—the former to the N.W, and *Sirius* (the brightest of all fixed stars) to the S E

In the same direction as, but further from the Belt than *Aldebaran*, is a notable cluster of small stars named the *Pleiades* These, though not actually useful for the purpose of navigation, afford a conspicuous mark for distinguishing neighbouring stars

The bright stars *Procyon*, *Betelguese*, and *Sirius* form an almost equilateral triangle, *Procyon* being to the Eastward of the others Nearly due North from *Procyon*, and about 23° from it, are the two stars *Castor* and *Pollux*

LEO.

This constellation may be found by following the "Pointers" in the Great Bear backwards, that is, in a direction opposite to the Pole Star

There is one very bright star in this group, viz, *Regulus* or α Leonis, and it is nearly equidistant from *Procyon* and *Pollux*, and to the Eastward of them Some of

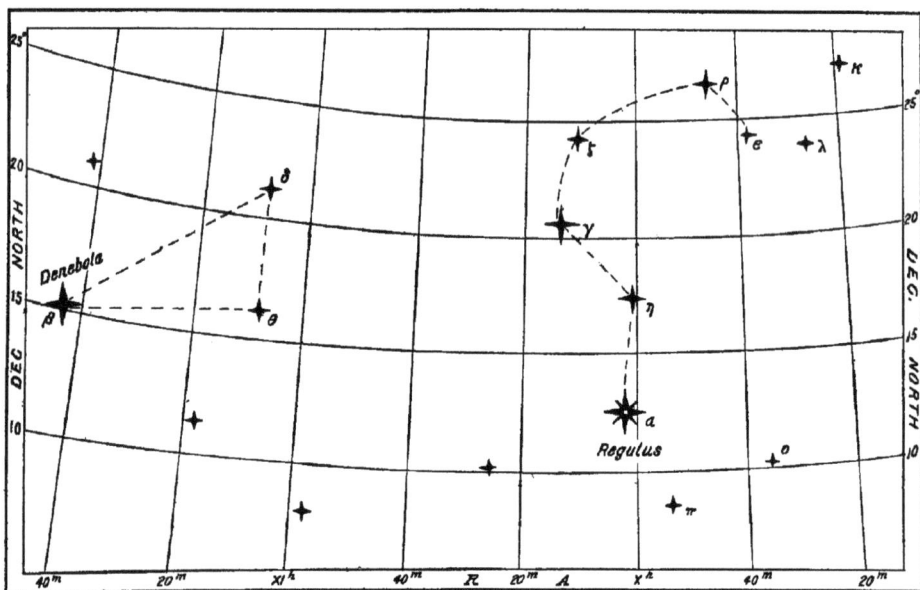

See also Large Map IV

the stars in LEO form the outline of a sickle, with *Regulus* at the handle Three other stars form a right-angled triangle β Leonis (*Denebola*), *Arcturus* and *Spica* form an almost equilateral triangle (*see* large map IV)

CYGNUS and LYRA.

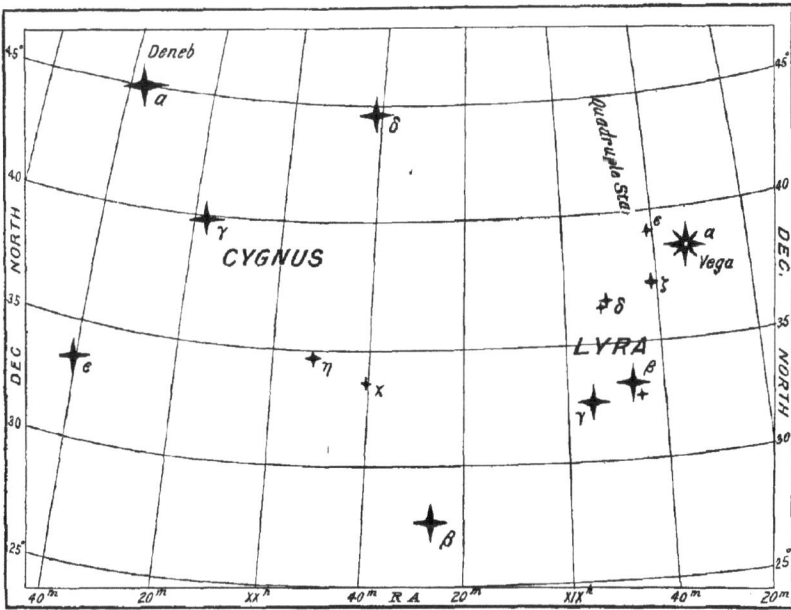

See also Large Map V

The principal star in LYRA is *Vega*, which may on a clear night be distinguished from the fact that it is the most brilliant star in this part of the heavens. From *Vega*, *Deneb* or α Cygni may be traced, also *Altair* (α Aquilæ) by comparing with map V or VI

A very useful way of identifying stars and planets by taking meridian altitudes, is explained further on

CRUX

(The Southern Cross).

There is no difficulty in identifying this constellation when above the horizon in the southern hemisphere Near it are the two stars α and β in CENTAURI

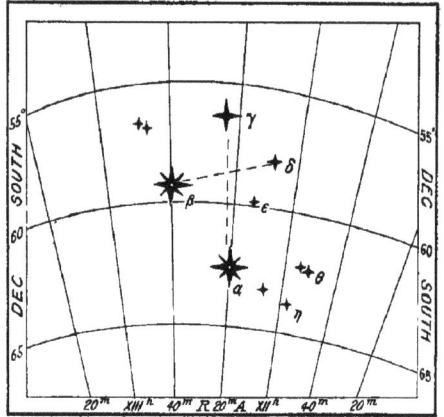

See also Large Map IV

THE PLANETS.

Hitherto attention has been directed to the *fixed* stars only   The relative positions of these with respect to each other, as seen from the earth, do not appreciably change, hence they are termed *fixed* stars

The planets (or wandering stars) are a number of bodies which revolve in orbits round the sun   Our own earth is one of these bodies, and the positions of the other planets as seen by us are constantly changing   The sun, together with the bodies which describe orbits round it, make up what is called the Solar System.

The fixed stars are at such an inconceivably immense distance from the Solar System, that, by comparison, the planets and the sun are relatively quite close to each other   The distance of the earth from the sun is calculated to be about 93,000,000 (ninety-three millions) of miles   This, of itself, is a distance which the mind cannot realise, but it shrinks into insignificance when compared with the distance of the nearest fixed star   To an imaginary observer on the nearest star this 93,000,000 of miles would only subtend an angle of about half-a-second of arc

The planets are not self-luminous bodies as are the sun and fixed stars   Their brightness is due to the light of the sun, which they reflect, resembling in this respect the moon

The principal planets are eight in number Their names, arranged in order of their distances from the sun, are *Mercury, Venus, Earth, Mars, Jupiter, Saturn, Uranus,* and *Neptune*

The navigator will find *Venus, Mars, Jupiter,* and *Saturn* most useful, and the R A and Declination of these four are given for every day in *Brown's Nautical Almanac*

The orbit of *Venus** round the sun is inside that of the earth. In consequence of this *Venus* appears to us to move from one side of the sun to the other, but never recedes further from it than about 47° When the R A of *Venus* exceeds that of the sun it will (if not too near it) become visible after sunset. If the R A. of *Venus* is less than that of the sun it will not be visible in the evening, but before sunrise in the morning

The brilliancy of the planets varies with their position Venus and Jupiter are so brilliant generally as to surpass the magnitude of any star The twinkling or flickering of the fixed stars is familiar to all, and at times this twinkling is more apparent than at others The planets do not twinkle so strongly as the stars , they shine with a much steadier light, and this fact helps the observer to distinguish them from the fixed stars

The position of a planet amongst the stars may be found at any time by taking its R A and Declination from the *Nautical Almanac* for the current date, and marking this point on one of the star maps, it can then be seen where it is situated amongst the stars.

It is interesting to observe the motion of the planets when they are visible, from night to night amongst the fixed stars

---

*The orbit of *Mercury* is also inside that of the earth, but being so near to the sun is not often visible to the naked eye.

PART II.

STAR PROBLEMS—With Examples

***

Right Ascension of the Meridian (R.A.M.)
or Sidereal Time at Ship.

THE SIDEREAL TIME at any place is the Westerly hour angle of the first point of Aries, and is identical with the Right Ascension of the Meridian

It is important in dealing with star problems to be able readily to find the R A M The following is the rule —

The *M S R A + Astronomical M T Ship = R A M or Sidereal Time at Ship
The   A S R A +   „   A.T Ship =   „   „   „

The rule may be more generally given thus —The Right Ascension of *any* object + its Westerly hour angle ˉ R A M

It is usually sufficiently exact to work to the nearest minute   The elements required may be taken from *Brown's Nautical Almanac*

***

*M S R A , an abbreviation for Mean Sun's Right Ascension
    A S R A ,   Apparent „

EXAMPLE I

1904, January 20th, at 6h 20m, a.m, M T. Ship, in longitude 80° E   What is
the R A M ?

Astronomical M T Ship,	D	H	M
	19	18	20
Longitude in Time,	0	5	20
M T G ,	19	13	0

		H	M
M S R A or Sidereal Time at			
noon at Greenwich on 19th,		19	50
Acceleration for 13hrs ,	+	0	2
Correction M.S.R.A ,		19	52
Astronomical M T Ship,		18	20
R A M ,		14	12

When the sum exceeds 24hrs reject the 24

EXAMPLE II

1904, July 18th, at 7h 28m P M , A T Ship, in longitude 153° E   What is the R A M ?

Astronomical A T Ship,	D	H	M
	18	7	28
Longitude E , −	0	10	12
A T G ,	17	21	16

		H	M
A S R A at noon at Greenwich			
on 17th,		= 7	45
Correction 21h 16m ,		+ 0	4
Correction A S R A ,		7	49
Astronomical A T. Ship,-		7	28
R A M ,		15	17

If the Almanad is not handy, a rough estimate of the sun's R A can be made
mentally by remembering that the sun's R A is 0 about the 22nd of March, increasing
2 hours per month, or about 4 minutes per day

To find what Bright Stars are near the Meridian.

This may be easily done by inspection from the maps   Get the R A M   Find
this meridian 'on one of the maps, and the stars lying near it will be those required
Those to the left will lie to the Eastward and are approaching, those to the right have
crossed the meridian.   In these problems it is hardly necessary to correct the sun's R A

Example I

1904, November 20th, at 1h 0m A M, M T at Ship   Find what bright stars are near
the meridian in latitude 48° N , longitude 30° W

	H	M
M T Ship (Astronomical),	13	·0
Approximate M S R A , +	16	14
R A M ,	5	14

Look at map II and note the meridian with R A 5 hours   The stars near it are—

Aldebaran to the West of the meridian and to the Southward of latitude

Capella nearly on meridian and almost overhead

Rigel nearly on meridian bearing South

Bellatrix and *Betelguese* to the Eastward of the meridian, and to the Southward of
the observer

All the aforementioned stars are within 1 hour of the meridian   *Aldebaran* has
already crossed, the others are approaching it

A more extensive list of stars near the meridian can be taken from the Table of
Stars (*see* page 4)   Stars with R A near the R A M are near the meridian   Those with
R A LESS than R A M are to the West of it, and those with GREATER R A are to the
East of the meridian   The above R A M 5h 14m (*see* Table of Stars on page 4), falls
between the R A of *Rigel* and *Bellatrix* both very close to the meridian

Rigel and those immediately above are near the meridian to the West

Bellatrix,   ,,   below   ,   ,,   ,,   East

Example II.

1904, June 11th at 8h 25m P M , A T at Ship, in latitude 30° S , longitude 120° W.
What bright stars are near the meridian?

	H	M
Astronomical A.T. Ship,	8	25
Approximate A S R A ,	5	20
R.A M ,	13	45

The stars near this meridian (*see* map IV) are—

Spica	West of the meridian and to the Northward.			
β Centauri	East	„	„	Southward
Arcturus	East	„	„	Northward
α Centauri	East	„	„	Southward

By looking at the Table of Stars for R A near 13h. 45m the names of one or two more near the meridian may be seen

To find the Time at which a Star will cross the Meridian.

For practical purposes at sea this can always be taken from tables. Most of the epitomes give tables of these, but those given in *Brown's Nautical Almanac* are corrected to date, and may be relied on as being accurate   In *Brown's Almanac* they are given for the 1st and every succeeding 5th day of each month   To find for any intermediate day, subtract 4 minutes for every day elapsed since the date given in the tables

On the same page in *Brown's Almanac* the meridian passage (termed Southing in the table) of the four planets Venus, Mars, Jupiter, and Saturn, for every third day of each month is given   It is easy to estimate the meridian passage for an intermediate day by proportion   These are also given for every day in the Admiralty Almanac.

The meridian passage of a star or planet may be calculated by subtracting the sun's R A for the given date from that of the object

Remarks on observing Star Altitudes.

In the actual observation of star altitudes the chief consideration is the visibility of the horizon line   The best time for taking an altitude is during twilight before sunrise or after sunset, when the horizon is clearly defined   The bright stars are so numerous that if the weather is clear there are always one or two that are in good position for observation during twilight, and the results obtained are in every way as reliable as if obtained from altitudes of the sun   Indeed, the very best method in fixing a ship's position at sea (both latitude and longitude) is afforded by taking simultaneous altitudes of two stars, as will be explained later

On moonlit nights also a good horizon may be obtained, but at other times some experience is required in order to judge of the reliability of the results   Constant practice will enable an observer to obtain good altitudes on dark clear nights, but at such times much will depend upon his keenness of vision, also the assistance of a good star telescope will then be useful   Efficiency, however, is only to be obtained by constant practice, and as experience is gained the observer will gradually get to know the amount of confidence that may be placed in an observation taken at any time

At first beginners should practice the bringing of a star down to the horizon without using a telescope   Put the index at o, and look through the telescope collar or ring and horizon glass direct at the star   Then gradually move the index along the arc, keeping the star's reflection in sight, and following it down until it reaches the horizon, when the index can be clamped and the contact made as perfect as possible   When meridian altitudes are required, it is easy to obtain the approximate altitude and clamp the index previous to observation , but, though this may be permissable at first, it is not recommended, as it is only applicable to stars when on the meridian

Latitude by Meridian Altitude of a Star.

This is the simplest of all methods of finding the latitude of a ship at sea   If the altitude is correctly observed, the finding of the latitude simply involves the addition or subtraction of a few figures   The time or longitude is not required to be known, and no correction for declination is necessary   Its simplicity recommends it to beginners, who will naturally make a start in stellar navigation by taking meridian altitudes   There is a constant succession of bright stars passing the meridian at short intervals, which afford frequent opportunities for practice with the sextant, and at the same time aids the observer in identifying and recognising the bright stars   Opportunities should be sought when the horizon is clear, and the results of several observations should be compared with each other, and also with the latitude by account. To know at what time the principal stars cross the meridian, the table giving the meridian passage of the stars may be consulted, and the star's approximate altitude computed for setting the sextant ready for observation

Suppose that on March 11th, 1904, at about 7h P M , in latitude by arc 19° 3′ N . it was required to find what bright stars would next be available for observing their meridian altitude, and also to find the approximate altitude for setting the sextant ready for observation   Height of eye 24 feet.

In turning to the table in *Brown's Almanac* or Norie's epitome, it is seen that the star Sirius will cross the meridian on March 11th about 7h 15m P M apparent time   Its approximate meridian altitude may be computed as under, by working a meridian altitude backwards

		°	′	
Lat. by acc ,	-	19	3 N.	
Sirius decl ,	- -	16	35 S	
Mer zen. dist.,	-	35	38	
		90	0	
Approx mer alt ,	- -	54	22	
Corr for dip and ref. reversed, +		0	5	(Table XV , Norie)
Approx alt for setting sextant, -		54	27	

The correction from Table XV , Norie, consists of the dip and refraction combined, which is always subtracted when computing the true altitude

With the index clamped at this reading, the observer, a few minutes before the time of the star's meridian passage, knowing from the star's declination that it is to the South, looks at the horizon in this direction through the horizon glass, when the reflection of the star will be seen in the horizon glass, and a good contact can be made by the tangent screw   Repeat this process at short intervals until its meridian altitude is obtained

Suppose the observer finds the observed meridian altitude of Sirius to be 54° 22′ bearing South, height of eye as before, the latitude is found as under —

Obs alt,	54	22 S
Corr for dip and ref,	− 0	5 (Table XV, None, or "Brown's Nautical Almanac.')
True alt,	− 54	17
	90	0
Zenith dist,	− 35	43 N
Decl of Sirius	− 16	35 S.
Latitude in,	19	8 N

It is a good plan to take the meridian altitudes of two stars that cross the meridian within a short time of each other, one bearing North and the other South By comparing the results, the observer will be able to test the accuracy of his observations

Latitude by Reduction to the Meridian.

In all ex-meridian problems time is an important factor   It is necessary that the correct time at ship (either mean or apparent) should be known   This may be found from a good watch whose error on apparent time at ship has been found from an observation of the sun during the day, or it may be obtained by applying the longitude in time to the mean time at Greenwich indicated by the chronometer   As, however, the observer may not have free access to a chronometer, the first method of finding the ship time will be used in the example shown here   Not only must the error of the watch be applied, but also a correction due to the difference of longitude made good since the error was determined, to be added if Easterly, and subtracted if Westerly   Stars near the zenith should not be used for this problem

EXAMPLE

1904, December 20th, P M at ship, in latitude by account 13° 32' N, longitude 86° 36' E, the observed altitude of the star Canopus when near the meridian was 23° 24', South of observer, height of eye 22 feet. The time by watch was 11h 58m 22s, which had been found during the day to be 5m 6s fast on apparent time at ship, and since this error was found the ship had made 13' difference of longitude to the Eastward. Required the latitude.

D long since
error was found—
13' E
4
—
in time = 52 secs

Long, 86° 36'
4
—
6,0)34,6 24
in time = 5ʰ 46ᵐ 24ˢ

		D	H	M	S
Time by watch, -	-	20	11	58	22
fast -				5	6
		20	11	53	16
D long E, -	+				52
Appt time ship,		20	11	54	8
Long E	—			5 46	24
Appt time Green,		20	6	7	44

		H	M	S
A S R A for Dec 20, -		17	52	11*
Corr for 6 1 hours,	-		1	8
Correct R.A,		17	53	19
A T ship, - -		11	54	8
R A M,		5	47	27
R A star,		6	21	53
Hour Angle of Canopus,			34	26 E.

Var 1 hour of
Sun's R A
11 10
6·1
—
1110
6660
—
6,0)67·710
1ᵐ 8ˢ

Obs alt,	- 23 24 S
Corr,	- 7
True alt.,	- 23 17
Red, -	+ 25
Merid alt,	23 42
	90 0
Zen dist,	- 66 18 N
Decl, -	- 52 38½ S.
Latitude,	- 13 39½ N

	M S.		
Hour angle,	34 26	Log	7 7508 (XXXI None)
Lat. by acc,	13° 32'N	Cos	9 9878
Decl,	- 52 38½ S	Cos	9 7830
E Z D,	- 66 10½	Cosec	10 0387
½ Red,	- 12' 29"	Sine	7·5603
	2		
	24 58		

---

* Work Time and Right Ascension to seconds in this problem

The Estimated Zenith Distance (E Z.D) is found by adding the latitude and Declination if they have different names, but by subtracting the less from the greater if they have the same name. The logs taken out to the first four decimals are sufficiently exact for practical purposes, but the sine of the half reduction should be taken out to the nearest second from the first pages of Table XXV., (Norie) Always add the reduction to the altitude, the result is then the meridian altitude which the star attains at the place of observation.

Latitude by Pole Star.

In Northern latitudes the Pole Star affords an easy method of finding the latitude.

First, the R A M or sidereal time at ship must be found.

Next, the star's true altitude must be obtained.

The latitude can then be found either by applying the corrections given in the tables at the end of the Nautical Almanac or by using the correction given in *Brown's Nautical Almanac*

EXAMPLE

1904, December 21st, at 1h 27m A M, M T at ship, in longitude 148° 54′ W, the observed altitude of the Pole Star was 39° 15′, height of eye 24 feet   Find the latitude.

	D	H	M
M T ship, -	20	13	27
Long in time W, +			9 56
M T G, - -	20	23	23

	H	M
M S R A 20th, -	17	54½
Corr for 23ʰ 23ᵐ, -		4
Corr M S R A,	17	58½
M T ship,	13	27
R A M,	7	25½

		°	′
Obs alt, -	-	39	15 N
Corr, -	-		6
True alt, -		39	9
Const, -	-		1
		39	8
Corr I, -			0
Corr II,	+		0½
Corr III,	+		1
Latitude, -	-	39	9½ N

Note —These corrections are taken from the Naut Almanac
    Leaving out both the constant and Corr. III can never
    make as much as one mile difference in the result, but
    do not omit one without also omitting the other

Time Azimuths of Stars.

The stars offer a particularly useful and easy means of ascertaining the deviation of the compass at night by time azimuths The altitude is not required, therefore it is immaterial whether the horizon is clear or not It is only necessary that the compass bearing be correctly observed, and the that the time of observation and the name of the star be known

Stars are in the best position for azimuth when not more than about 30° from the horizon Burdwood's Time Azimuth Tables (for latitudes 30° to 60° N or S) and Davis's (for latitudes 0° to 30° N or S) can be used for any star whose declination does not exceed 23°, by following the rules below. The observer who has studied the maps and directions in Part I should have no difficulty in selecting a suitable star for these tables, and whenever an azimuth is required to be taken there are almost sure to be one or two in a good position for observation

Before proceeding to work out an example it will be necessary to give the rules for finding a star's hour angle from the time at ship

First find the R A M

Under it place the star's R A , the difference between them is the star's hour angle Then —

If the R A. has been subtracted from the R A.M., name the angle hour W

,, R A M ,,   ,,   ,,   R.A.   ,,   ,,   E

If the hour angle should exceed 12 hours subtract it from 24 and change its name

When using the tables always look for the star's hour angle in the column at the right hand margin of the page (under P M)

Always name the true azimuth the same as the latitude, and the same as the hour angle.

EXAMPLE

1904, June 19th, at 1h 20m A M, A T at Ship   Position by D R latitude 42° S,
longitude 131° E , the star β Ceti bore by compass E ¼ N   Find the error and
deviation of the compass for the course the ship was steering, the variation from
the chart being 3° W

	D H M			H M	FROM BURDWOOD'S TABLES
A T ship,	18 13 20	A S R A 18th, =		5 46	Lat, 42° S ⎫ True az, S 80°½ E.
Long E, -	8 44	Corr for 4½ hrs,		1	Star's Decl, 18°½ S ⎬ 180°
A T Green, 18 4 36		A T ship,		13 20	,, H A, 5ʰ 32ᵐ E ⎭
		R A M,		19 7	True az, N 99°½ E
		Star's R A,		0 39	Obs az, N 81°½ E
		Star's H Angle,-	18 28 W.		Error, 18° E
			24 0		Var, 3° W
		Hour Angle,		5 32 E	Dev, 21° E

Longitude by Chronometer from an Altitude of a Star.

The observer is supposed to be already familiar with the method of finding the
longitude from an observation of the sun   When a star has been observed, its hour
angle is calculated in the same manner as the sun's, after which, proceed as follows —

If the hour angle is W , add it to the star's R A

If the hour angle is E , subtract it from 24 hours and then add to the star's R A *
    The sum in either case will be the R A M

From the R A M , + 24 hours if required, subtract the M S R A (corrected for the
    M T Green), the remainder is the M T ship   Prefix to it the astronomical
    date at ship, that is the same day as civil date if P M , but previous day if A.M.

Under the M T ship place the M T Green , their difference is the longitude in
    time which must then be changed into arc

Stars nearest to the prime vertical should be chosen for finding longitude

---

* In this rule the star's hour angle is supposed to have been taken from the top of the hour angle table

EXAMPLE

1904, March 24th, A M. at ship, in latitude 19° 42′ S , the observed altitude of the star α Bootis (Arcturus) after passing the meridian was 25° 1′, height of eye 24 feet The astronomical time by chronometer was 23d 11h 44m 36s, which was fast 2m 17s on M T G   Required the longitude

	D	H	M	S				·	′
Chronometer Time,	23	11	44	36		Star's decl ,	-	19	41 N
Fast,	—		2	17				90	0
M.T.G ,	23	11	42	19		Polar dist ,		109	41

		°	′				
Obs. alt.,	-	25	1	Alt ,	24 54		
Diff and Ref ,	—	7		Lat	19 42	Sec	10 02619
True alt ,		24	54	P D ,	109 41	Cosec.	10 02615

		H	M	S				
					2)154 17			
M S R A 23rd,		0	2	11	½ sum	77 8½	Cos	9 34741
Corr 11ʰ 42ᵐ			1	55	Rem ,	52 14½	Sin	9 89796
Correct M S.R.A.,	0	4	6					9 29771.

			H	M	S
Star's W'ly H angle,			3	31	39
Star's R A ,		-	14	11	18
R A.M ,	-	-	17	42	57
M S R A ,	-		0	4	6
M T ship, 23rd,	-	-	17	38	51
M.T. Green., 23rd,		-	11	42	19
			5	56	32
			60		
		4)356	32		
	Longitude	89	8 E		

If a planet's altitude is observed proceed exactly as above, using the planet's declination and right ascension, first correcting them for the mean time at Greenwich

Ship's Position by Simultaneous Altitudes of Two Stars.

By observing the altitudes of two stars at twilight whilst the horizon is clear, it is possible to determine the ship's position with great accuracy   This is probably the best method of finding the position by observation, as the latitude and longitude can both be determined at once, without waiting (as must be done when the sun is observed) for the necessary change of bearing   In selecting two stars it must be noted that the nearer their bearings are to forming a right angle with each other the more reliable the result will be, and that stars very near the zenith should not be chosen

The observer is supposed to be familiar with the method and principle of finding the ship's position from two altitudes of the sun with two assumed latitudes by Sumner's method   The same method might easily be applied to the simultaneous altitudes of two stars, but the general modern method is to assume one latitude only—i e , the latitude by D R —as a basis, and with it determine a longitude from each of the observations If these two longitudes agree, it is the true longitude of the ship, and the latitude used is also the true latitude, and the ship's position is known without further calculation. Generally, however, the two longitudes will differ, proving that the latitude assumed is in error   It is evident that the greater the error in the assumed latitude, the greater will be the difference between the resulting longitudes   It is then necessary to find out how much the assumed latitude is in error, and thence obtain the true longitude   There are many ways in which this may be done   Johnson's method may be used with advantage, and can be recommended for practical use at sea

Another good method is that in which the A and B tables are employed   For a full explanation of both these methods the observer is referred to the books specially dealing with them, which also contain the necessary tables   The purpose of this book will be best served by a worked example in which the true position is found by projection, as being more instructive, very simple, and forming a very good introduction to the study of the methods already mentioned   There are practically no rules to remember.   The true bearing of each star at the time of observation is obtained from the Azimuth Tables, the lines of position must be at right angles to these bearings, and the intersection of these lines of position, drawn through the corresponding points on the chart, must be the ship's position

EXAMPLE

1904, April 22nd, about 8h 20m P.M., M T at ship, position by D.R., latitude 42° 10′ N, longitude 11° W, the following altitudes of two stars were taken simultaneously Observed altitude of Sirius West of meridian 12° 51′, observed altitude of Arcturus East of meridian 36° 56′; height of eye 23 feet The chronometer indicated 9h 3m 30s, M T Greenwich Required the true position by observation

Sirius, West of Meridian.

	D. H M S				H M S
M T G., -	22 9 3 30	Star's R A,	6 40 55		

	H M S		° ′ ″		° ′
M S R A,	2 0 27	Decl, -	- 16 35 24 S	Obs alt,	- 12 51
Corr	+ 1 29		90 0 0	Corr,	— 9
M S R A,	2 1 56	P D., -	106 35 24	True alt,	- 12 42

	° ′						H M S
Alt, -	22 42			Star's W'ly H angle,			3 38 20
Lat,	42 10	Sec.	0 13007	Star's R A,			6 40 55
P D,	106 35½	Cosec	0 01847	R A M,			10 19 15
	2)171 27½			M S R A,			2 1 56
	80 44	Cos	9 20691	M T ship, 22nd,			8 17 19
	68 2	Sin	9 96727	M T Green, 22nd,	-		9 3 30
3ʰ 38ᵐ 20ᵏ			9·32272			4)46 11	

Longitude A, 11° 32′ 45″W.

With latitude 42° N, declination 16½ S, hour angle 3h 38m W, the true azimuth of Sirius from the tables is S 53° W The line of position must be at right angles to this, and therefore runs N 37° W and S 37° E

Mark the position of latitude 42° 10′ N, longitude 11° 32¾′ W, on the chart, and through it draw a line of position as above (*see* line *A C* in the figure).

Arcturus, East of Meridian.

Star's R A ,	14 11 19 (H M S)		

Decl ,	- 19 40 49 N. (° ′ ″)		Obs alt ,	-	- 36 56 (° ′)	
	90 0 0		Corr ,	-	- - 6	
P D ,	70 19 11		True alt ,		36 50	

			H M S.
Star's E'ly H angle,	-		3 50 37
			24 0 0
Star's W'ly H angle,			20 9 23
Star's R A ,			14 11 19
R A M ,			10 20 42
M S R A ,			2 1 56
M T ship,	22nd,		8 18 46
M T G ,	22nd,		9 3 30
			4)44 44
Longitude B , 11 11 W			

Alt ,	36 50 (° ′)		
Lat ,	42 10	Sec	0 13007
P D ,	70 19	Cosec	0 02615
Sum,	149 19		
Half, -	74 39½	Cos	9 42255
Rem ,	37 49½	Sin	9 78764
3ʰ 50ᵐ 37ˢ			9 36641

With latitude 42° N , declination 20° N , hour angle 3h 50m E., the true azimuth of Arcturus from the tables is found to be S 84° E   The corresponding line of position is therefore N 6° E and S 6° W

Mark the point B in latitude 42° 10′ N , longitude 11° 11′ W., on the chart, and through it draw this line of position   The point where it cuts the other line is the position of the ship

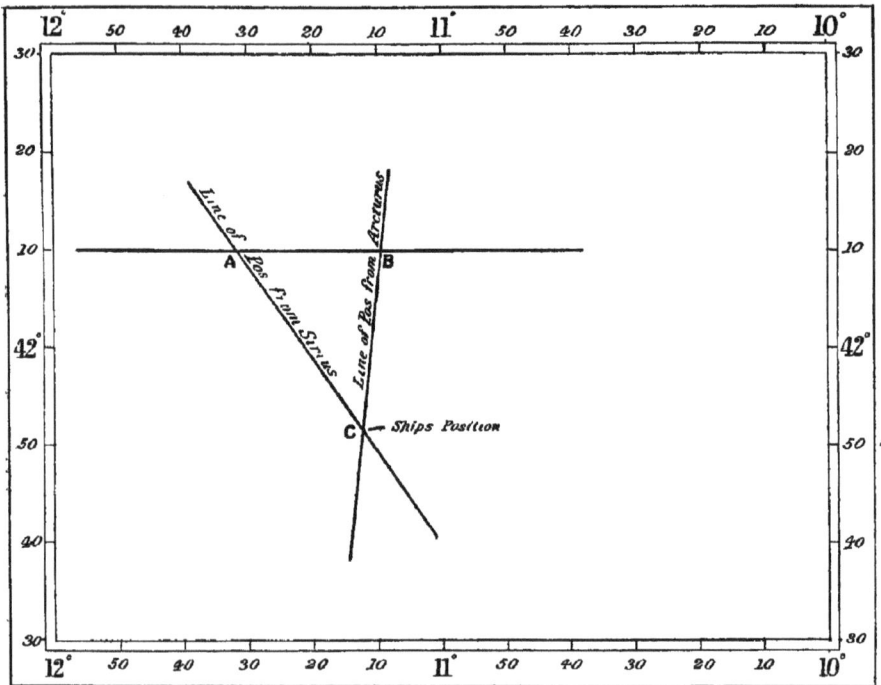

Ship's true position, latitude 41° 51½′ N , longitude 11° 14′ W.

The simultaneous altitudes of a star and a planet, or of two planets, may be dealt with in a similar manner. When a planet is observed, its R.A and declination must be corrected for the mean time at Greenwich

If a star is observed whose declination exceeds 23°, its azimuth cannot be taken from Burdwood's or Davis's Tables, but it can be found by the A, B, and C Tables in Norie. Also the time azimuth tables do not give the azimuths where the altitude exceeds 60°.

SPECIAL CASE—The work may be considerably abbreviated in the particular case when the star is on or near the meridian The latitude should then be first calculated by meridian altitude or reduction to the meridian as the case may be This latitude may then be used for finding the longitude by chronometer from the altitude of the other star.

when the horizon is clear, and the results of several observations should be compared with each other, and also with the latitude by account   To know at what time the principal stars cross the meridian, the table giving the meridian passage of the stars may be consulted, and the star's approximate altitude computed for setting the sextant ready for observation

Suppose that on March 11th, 1904, at about 7h. P.M., in latitude by arc 19° 3′ N, it was required to find what bright stars would next be available for observing their meridian altitude, and also to find the approximate altitude for setting the sextant ready for observation   Height of eye 24 feet

In turning to the table in *Brown's Almanac* or Norie's epitome, it is seen that the star Sirius will cross the meridian on March 11th about 7h 15m P M apparent time   Its approximate meridian altitude may be computed as under, by working a meridian altitude backwards

			°	′	
Lat by acc.,	-	-	-	19	3 N.
Sirius decl ,	-		16	35 S	
Mer. zen dist ,	-		35	38	
			90	0	
Approx mer alt ,	-	-	54	22	
Corr. for dip and ref reversed, +		0	5	(Table XV , Norie)	
Approx alt for setting sextant,		54	27		

The correction from Table XV., Norie, consists of the dip and refraction combined, which is always subtracted when computing the true altitude

With the index clamped at this reading, the observer, a few minutes before the time of the star's meridian passage, knowing from the star's declination that it is to the South, looks at the horizon in this direction through the horizon glass, when the reflection of the star will be seen in the horizon glass, and a good contact can be made by the tangent screw   Repeat this process at short intervals until its meridian altitude is obtained

Suppose the observer finds the observed meridian altitude of Sirius to be
54° 22′ bearing South, height of eye as before, the latitude is found as under —

			°	′	
Obs. alt ,	- -	-	54	22 S.	
Corr for dip and ref ,		– 0		5	(Table XV , None, or " Brown's Nautical Almanac ')
True alt ,			54	17	
			90	0	
Zenith dist ,		-	35	43 N	
Decl of Sirius	-		16	35 S	
Latitude in,			19	8 N	

It is a good plan to take the meridian altitudes of two stars that cross the
meridian within a short time of each other, one bearing North and the other South.
By comparing the results, the observer will be able to test the accuracy of his
observations

Latitude by Reduction to the Meridian.

In all ex-meridian problems time is an important factor   It is necessary that the
correct time at ship (either mean or apparent) should be known   This may be found
from a good watch whose error on apparent time at ship has been found from an
observation of the sun during the day, or it may be obtained by applying the longitude
in time to the mean time at Greenwich indicated by the chronometer   As, however, the
observer may not have free access to a chronometer, the first method of finding the
ship time will be used in the example shown here   Not only must the error of the
watch be applied, but also a correction due to the difference of longitude made good
since the error was determined, to be added if Easterly, and subtracted if Westerly   Stars
near the zenith should not be used for this problem

EXAMPLE

1904, December 20th, P M at ship, in latitude by account 13° 32′ N , longitude 86° 36′ E , the observed altitude of the star Canopus when near the meridian was 23° 24′, South of observer, height of eye 22 feet The time by watch was 11h 58m 22s, which had been found during the day to be 5m 6s fast on apparent time at ship, and since this error was found the ship had made 13′ difference of longitude to the Eastward Required the latitude.

D long since error was found— 13′ E 4		
in time = 52 secs		
Long , 86° 36′ 4		
6,0)34,6 24		
in time = 5ʰ 46ᵐ 24ˢ		

	D	H	M	S		H	M	S
Time by watch,	- 20	11	58	22	A S R A for Dec 20, =	17	52	11*
fast -			5	6	Corr for 6 1 hours, -		1	8
	20	11	53	16	Correct R A ,	17	53	19
D long E +				52	A T ship, -	11	54	8
Appt time ship, - 20		11	54	8	R A M , -	5	47	27
Long E -			5	46 24	R A star,	6	21	53
Appt time Green ,	20	6	7 44		Hour Angle of Canopus,		34	26 E

Var 1 hour of Sun's R A 11 10 6 1 1110 6660 6,0)67 710 1ᵐ 8ˢ	Obs alt , - 23 24 S		

	° ′		
Obs alt ,	- 23 24 S		
Corr ,	- 7	Hour angle, 34 26	Log 7 750S (XXXI None)
True alt ,	23 17	Lat by acc , 13° 32′N	Cos 9 9878
Red , -	+ 25	Decl , 52 38½ S	Cos 9 7830
Merid alt ,	23 42	E.Z D , 66 10½	Cosec 10 0387
	90 0	½ Red , - 12′ 29″	Sine 7 5603
Zen dist ,	- 66 18 N	2	
Decl , -	52 38½ S	24 58	
Latitude,	- 13 39½ N.		

M S (above Hour angle: 34 26), (above Decl: 52 38½ S), (above E.Z D: 66 10½), (above ½ Red: 12′ 29″)

---

* Work Time and Right Ascension to seconds in this problem

The Estimated Zenith Distance (E Z D) is found by adding the latitude and Declination if they have different names, but by subtracting the less from the greater if they have the same name   The logs taken out to the first four decimals are sufficiently exact for practical purposes, but the sine of the half reduction should be taken out to the nearest second from the first pages of Table XXV, (Norie)   Always add the reduction to the altitude ; the result is then the meridian altitude which the star attains at the place of observation

Latitude by Pole Star.

In Northern latitudes the Pole Star affords an easy method of finding the latitude
First, the R A M or sidereal time at ship must be found.
Next, the star's true altitude must be obtained

The latitude can then be found either by applying the corrections given in the tables at the end of the Nautical Almanac or by using the correction given in *Brown's Nautical Almanac.*

EXAMPLE.

1904, December 21st, at 1h 27m A M , M T at ship, in longitude 148° 54′ W , the observed altitude of the Pole Star was 39° 15′, height of eye 24 feet   Find the latitude.

	D	H	M
M T ship, -	20	13	27
Long in time W, +		9	56
M T G , -	20	23	23

	H	M
M S R A 20th, -	17	54½
Corr for 23ʰ 23ᵐ , -		4
Corr M S R A , -	17	58½
M T ship, - -	13	27
R A M , -	7	25½

		°	′
Obs alt., -	-	39	15 N.
Corr ,	-		6
True alt ,		39	9
Const , -	-		1
		39	8
Corr I , -			0
Corr II ,	- +		0½
Corr III ,	+		1
Latitude, -	-	39	9½N

Note —These corrections are taken from the Naut Almanac
Leaving out both the constant and Corr III can never make as much as one mile difference in the result, but do not omit one without also omitting the other

Time Azimuths of Stars.

The stars offer a particularly useful and easy means of ascertaining the deviation of the compass at night by time azimuths The altitude is not required, therefore it is immaterial whether the horizon is clear or not It is only necessary that the compass bearing be correctly observed, and the that the time of observation and the name of the star be known

Stars are in the best position for azimuth when not more than about 30° from the horizon Burdwood's Time Azimuth Tables (for latitudes 30° to 60° N or S) and Davis's (for latitudes 0° to 30° N or S) can be used for any star whose declination does not exceed 23°, by following the rules below The observer who has studied the maps and directions in Part I should have no difficulty in selecting a suitable star for these tables, and whenever an azimuth is required to be taken there are almost sure to be one or two in a good position for observation.

Before proceeding to work out an example it will be necessary to give the rules for finding a star's hour angle from the time at ship

First find the R A M

Under it place the star's R A , the difference between them is the star's hour angle Then —

If the R A has been subtracted from the R A M , name the angle hour W

„ R A M. „   „   „   R A   „   „   E

If the hour angle should exceed 12 hours subtract it from 24 and change its name

When using the tables always look for the star's hour angle in the column at the right hand margin of the page (under P M)

Always name the true azimuth the same as the latitude, and the same as the hour angle

EXAMPLE

1904, June 19th, at 1h. 20m A M, A T. at Ship   Position by D R latitude 42° S ,
longitude 131° E , the star β Ceti bore by compass E. $\frac{3}{4}$ N.   Find the error and
deviation of the compass for the course the ship was steering, the variation from
the chart being 3° W

		D H M			H M	

FROM BURDWOOD'S TABLES

A T ship,   18 13 20   A S R A 18th, = 5 46
Long E ,   –   8 44   Corr for 4½ hrs ,   1   Lat , -   42° S ⎫ True az , S 80°½ E
                                                         Star's Decl , 18°½ S ⎬   180°
A T Green , 18 4 36   A T ship,   13 20   „ H.A , 5ʰ 32ᵐ E ⎭
                           R A M ,   19 7   True az , N 99°½ E.
                           Star's R A ,   0 39   Obs. az , N 81°½ E
                           Stars H Angle,- 18 28 W   Error,   18° E
                                            24 0   Var ,   3° W
                           Hour Angle,   5 32 E   Dev ,   21° E

Longitude by Chronometer from an Altitude of a Star.

The observer is supposed to be already familiar with the method of finding the
longitude from an observation of the sun   When a star has been observed, its hour
angle is calculated in the same manner as the sun's, after which, proceed as follows —

If the hour angle is W , add it to the star's R A

If the hour angle is E , subtract it from 24 hours and then add to the star's R A [*]
The sum in either case will be the R A M

From the R A M , + 24 hours if required, subtract the M S.R.A. (corrected for the
M T Green), the remainder is the M T ship   Prefix to it the astronomical
date at ship, that is the same day as civil date if P M , but previous day if A M.

Under the M T ship place the M T Green , their difference is the longitude in
time which must then be changed into arc

Stars nearest to the prime vertical should be chosen for finding longitude

---

[*] In this rule the star's hour angle is supposed to have been taken from the top of the hour angle table

EXAMPLE

1904, March 24th. A M at ship, in latitude 19° 42′ S, the observed altitude of the star a Bootis (Arcturus) after passing the meridian was 25° 1′, height of eye 24 feet The astronomical time by chronometer was 23d 11h 44m 36s, which was fast 2m 17s on M T G   Required the longitude

	D	H	M	S			°	′	
Chronometer Time,	23	11	44	36		Star's decl ,	-	19	41 N
Fast,	-	—	2	17				90	0
M T G , -	23	11	42	19		Polar dist ,		109	41

	°	′			°	′	
Obs. alt., -	25	1	Alt ,	24	54		
Diff. and Ref.,	—	7	Lat.	19	42	Sec	10 02619
True alt ,	24	54	P D ,	109	41	Cosec	10 02615
				2)154	17		
	H	M	S				
M S R.A 23rd,	0	2	11	½ sum	77	8½	Cos	9 34741
Corr 11ʰ 42ᵐ -		1	55	Rem.,	52	14½	Sin	9 89796
Correct M S R A.,	0	4	6					9 29771

	H	M	S
Star's W'ly H angle,	3	31	39
Star's R A , -	14	11	18
R A M , - -	17	42	57
M S R A ,	0	4	6
M T ship, 23rd, -	17	38	51
M T. Green , 23rd,	11	42	19
	5	56	32
	60		
	4)356	32	
Longitude	89	8 E	

If a planet's altitude is observed proceed exactly as above, using the planet's declination and right ascension, first correcting them for the mean time at Greenwich

Ship's Position by Simultaneous Altitudes of Two Stars.

By observing the altitudes of two stars at twilight whilst the horizon is clear, it is possible to determine the ship's position with great accuracy   This is probably the best method of finding the position by observation, as the latitude and longitude can both be determined at once, without waiting (as must be done when the sun is observed) for the necessary change of bearing   In selecting two stars it must be noted that the nearer their bearings are to forming a right angle with each other the more reliable the result will be, and that stars very near the zenith should not be chosen

The observer is supposed to be familiar with the method and principle of finding the ship's position from two altitudes of the sun with two assumed latitudes by Sumner's method   The same method might easily be applied to the simultaneous altitudes of two stars, but the general modern method is to assume one latitude only—*i e*, the latitude by D R —as a basis, and with it determine a longitude from each of the observations If these two longitudes agree, it is the true longitude of the ship, and the latitude used is also the true latitude, and the ship's position is known without further calculation. Generally, however, the two longitudes will differ, proving that the latitude assumed is in error.   It is evident that the greater the error in the assumed latitude, the greater will be the difference between the resulting longitudes   It is then necessary to find out how much the assumed latitude is in error, and thence obtain the true longitude   There are many ways in which this may be done   Johnson's method may be used with advantage, and can be recommended for practical use at sea

Another good method is that in which the A and B tables are employed.   For a full explanation of both these methods the observer is referred to the books specially dealing with them, which also contain the necessary tables   The purpose of this book will be best served by a worked example in which the true position is found by projection, as being more instructive, very simple, and forming a very good introduction to the study of the methods already mentioned   There are practically no rules to remember.   The true bearing of each star at the time of observation is obtained from the Azimuth Tables, the lines of position must be at right angles to these bearings, and the intersection of these lines of position, drawn 'through the corresponding points on the chart, must be the ship's position

EXAMPLE

1904, April 22nd, about 8h. 20m P M , M.T. at ship, position by D R., latitude 42° 10′ N , longitude 11° W , the following altitudes of two stars were taken simultaneously Observed altitude of Sirius West of meridian 12° 51′, observed altitude of Arcturus East of meridian 36° 56′, height of eye 23 feet   The chronometer indicated 9h 3m 30s , M T Greenwich   Required the true position by observation

Sirius, West of Meridian.

	D.	H	M.	S										
M T G , -	22	9	3	30	Star's R A ,			H 6	M 40	S 55				

		H	M	S			°	′	″				°	′
M.S.R.A.,		2	0	27	Decl , -		16	35	24 S	Obs alt , -			12	51
Corr		+	1	29			90	0	0	Corr.,			−	9
M S R A ,		2	1	56	P D , -		106	35	24	True alt ,			12	42

	°	′						H	M	S
Alt ,	22	42			Star's W'ly H angle,			3	38	20
Lat ,	42	10	Sec	0 13007	Star's R A ,	-		6	40	55
P D ,	106	35½	Cosec	0 01847	R A M ,			10	19	15
	2)171	27½			M S R.A.,			2	1	56
	80	44	Cos	9 20691	M T ship, 22nd,	-		8	17	19
	68	2	Sin	9 96727	M T Green , 22nd,		-	9	3	30
3ʰ 38ᵐ 20ˢ				9·32272				4)46	11	

Longitude A, 11° 32′ 45″ W

With latitude 42° N., declination 16½ S., hour angle 3h 38m. W , the true azimuth of Sirius from the tables is S 53° W   The line of position must be at right angles to this, and therefore runs N 37° W and S. 37° E

Mark the position of latitude 42° 10′ N , longitude 11° 32¾′ W , on the chart, and through it draw a line of position as above (*see* line **A C** in the figure)

Arcturus, East of Meridian.

Star's R A ,	H M S 14 11 19

Decl ,	' " 19 40 49 N		Obs. alt.,	- -	° ' 36 56
	90 0 0		Corr ,	- - -	6
P D ,	70 19 11		True alt ,		36 50

		H M S
Star's E'ly H angle,	- -	3 50 37
		24 0 0
Star's W'ly H angle,		20 9 23
Star's R A ,		14 11 19

	° '		
Alt ,	36 50		
Lat ,	42 10	Sec	0 13007
P D ,	70 19	Cosec	0 02615
Sum,	- 149 19		
Half,	74 39½	Cos	9 42255
Rem ,	37 49½	Sin	9 78764
	3ʰ 50ᵐ 37ˢ		9 36641

R A M ,		10 20 42
M S R A ,		2 1 56
M T ship,	22nd,	8 18 46
M T G , -	22nd,	9 3 30
		4)44 44
Longitude B , 11 11 W		

With latitude 42° N , declination 20° N , hour angle 3h 50m E , the true azimuth of Arcturus from the tables is found to be S 84° E   The corresponding line of position is therefore N 6° E and S. 6° W

Mark the point B in latitude 42° 10' N, longitude 11° 11' W, on the chart, and through it draw this line of position   The point where it cuts the other line is the position of the ship.

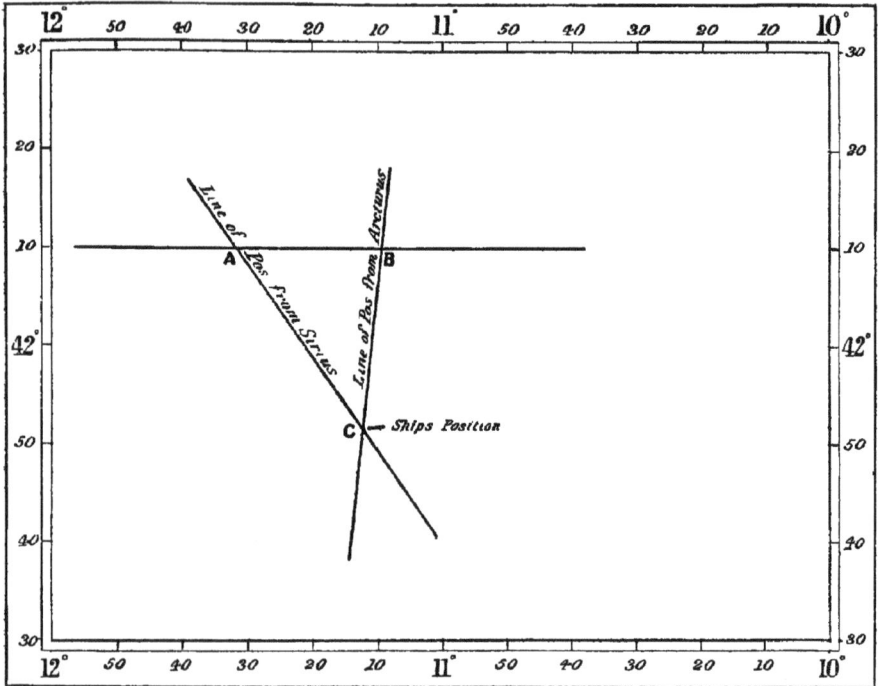

Ship's true position, latitude 41° 51½' N , longitude 11° 14' W

The simultaneous altitudes of a star and a planet, or of two planets, may be dealt with in a similar manner   When a planet is observed, its R A. and declination must be corrected for the mean time at Greenwich

If a star is observed whose declination exceeds 23°, its azimuth cannot be taken from Burdwood's or Davis's Tables, but it can be found by the A, B, and C Tables in Norie   Also the time azimuth tables do not give the azimuths where the altitude exceeds 60°.

SPECIAL CASE —The work may be considerably abbreviated in the particular case when the star is on or near the meridian   The latitude should then be first calculated by meridian altitude or reduction to the meridian as the case may be   This latitude may then be used for finding the longitude by chronometer from the altitude of the other star

Lightning Source UK Ltd.
Milton Keynes UK
UKHW020632170822
407432UK00006B/943

9 781375 890342